First published in Great Britain in 2009
by Piccadilly Press Ltd,
5 Castle Road, London NW1 8PR
www.piccadillypress.co.uk

Text copyright © Beatrice Masini, 2006
English language translation © Laura Watkinson 2009
Translated from the original *Il Mondo del Balletto*,
published by Edizioni El, Trieste, Italy
www.edizioniel.com
Illustrations copyright © Sara Not 2006
Published by arrangement with Rights People, London

A catalogue record for this book is available
from the British Library

ISBN: 978 1 84812 036 5

Printed and bound in China by WKT
Cover design by Patrick Knowles
Cover illustration by Sara Not

Beatrice Masini

Sara Not

The World of Ballet

Translated by Laura Watkinson

Piccadilly Press · London

I'm not sure what I want to be when I grow up . . .

Right now, I'm twelve, and I'm studying
classical dance at The Academy. Sometimes it can be hard
work, but usually it's great fun! Sometimes I don't have the slightest
doubt and I know for sure that I'm going to be a ballerina when I'm older.
But there's more to being a ballerina than just wanting to be one. It all depends
on how talented you are and it's still too soon for me to tell. There are times when
I think I'd rather be a writer, but I still have loads of time to make up my mind.
Anyway, I thought it would be a great idea to combine the two and write about the world
of dance and how I see it. Because there's so much to talk about, I've asked some of my
friends to help. Some of them are my age and some of them are grown-ups. Some are
already working in the world of dance, while others are still dreaming about it. But
all of them know a lot about particular parts of this world. And if you put all of those
different parts together, you complete the picture. Dance isn't like a normal
picture, though – it's a living picture, always moving, always different.
And I'm really happy that I'm part of that picture.

Kai
Zwerger

Madame
Olenska

Gimenez

Alissa

Roberto

Lucas

WHAT TO WEAR

Every aspiring ballerina
wants to wear a tutu.
But they have
to wait a long time!

ballerina black

ballerina blue

ballerina pink

As Madame Olenska always says, dance isn't all about satin and sequins; it's about practice and hard work. And when you're training, the best thing to wear is a simple leotard in stretch cotton – it hugs your body and adapts to your movements. You can have one with short sleeves or three-quarter-length sleeves, maybe with just the tiniest hint of a frill or even a little wraparound skirt. The colours are very simple too: black, blue or pink.

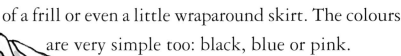

The boys' outfits are also simple. They wear a white T-shirt and black leggings or stretchy shorts.

In some schools, the students wear a sort of tracksuit when they're going between the changing rooms and the dance studio. It keeps you warm and stops you from catching cold. Cardigans and legwarmers are almost as good, can look wonderful and make you feel like a professional ballerina, so it can be hard to resist the temptation, especially when they're pink and fluffy, like little clouds!

You also need a special bag for all of your dance things, so it will have to be big and strong. Lots of dancers even use a small suitcase with wheels so that they don't have to carry a heavy bag around on their back.

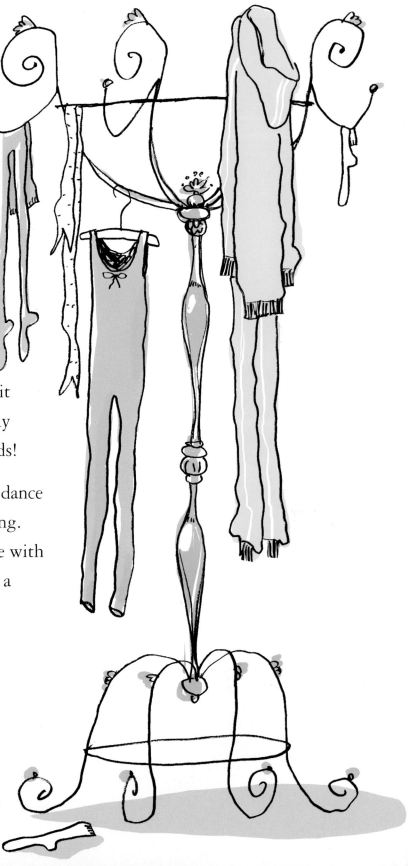

BALLET SHOES

You do your first ballet lessons in bare feet, or close enough!

All you need at the very start is a pair of socks or soft ballet slippers. When you first start dancing, you need to learn how to use your body, and your feet are a very important part of that. Going almost barefoot teaches your feet that they have to work really hard.

When you get to a certain stage, you may start wearing demi-pointe shoes. These are made from very soft leather or cloth and are held on with a strip of elastic or cotton laces. They're usually pink. They have a very supple sole, compared with normal shoes, and a soft block in the toe section to prepare you for proper pointe shoes. Boys have white or black shoes with a strip of elastic to hold them on. You wear these demi-pointe shoes for folk dances, or sometimes a different design with small heels and a strap.

If a floor is very slippery, you can dust the soles of your shoes with rosin powder so that you don't slip.

It takes a few years of practice before young ballerinas are ready to move on to pointe shoes. The tip of pointe shoes is a kind of box made of layers of fabric and glue, and it works as a small platform to support the weight of the body. The outer part of the shoe is made of satin, including the ribbons. The shoes are quite delicate and the satin sometimes gets damaged when it brushes the floor. It can be hard to get used to wearing pointe shoes at first. They can really hurt your feet.

Some ballerinas wear out one pair of shoes – or even more! – for every show they dance in. Every ballerina takes great pride in looking after her shoes and has her own little tricks for making them as comfortable as possible.

With pointe shoes, you wear thick powder-coloured or flesh-coloured tights, which are made specially for ballerinas.

You have to buy all of these items of clothing from specialist dance shops. The socks and tights that you buy in ordinary shops are no good for dancing. Besides, dance shops are wonderful places to visit – you can go along and have a peep at all the lovely things that you might get to wear one day!

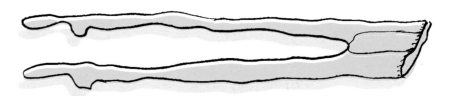

HOW TO WEAR YOUR HAIR

Ballerinas put their hair up so that it doesn't get in the way.

It's good to grow your hair to a length where it at least reaches your shoulders.
This makes it easier to put into a ponytail, and then into a bun,
and fix the ends with hairgrips.

Fringes also have to be pinned up and tamed with grips.
Lots of ballerinas don't have a fringe, though –
it's easier to tie up hair that's all the same length.

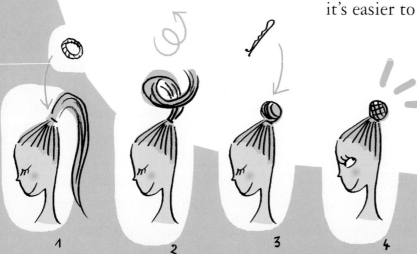

1   2   3   4

If you want to make a bun in your hair, start by combing your hair into a high ponytail, and fix it with a hairband. Then you wrap your hair around the hairband and fix the bun in place with grips. Finally, you can wrap a hairnet around the bun to keep it together and stop any stray pieces of hair from escaping.

Lots of schools also allow girls to put their hair in plaits for lessons. If your hair is too short to put up, you can use a headband to hold it back. The important thing is to follow the school rules.

Every ballerina has a beauty case packed with elastic bands, hairgrips, nets and hairbrushes.

For performances, ballerinas wear ribbons and flowers in their hair or tiaras and crowns to match their costumes. But for everyday life at dance school, simplicity is the rule.

GETTING READY FOR THE LESSON

First of all, off with the jewellery!

No earrings, rings, necklaces or bracelets are allowed. It's best just to leave them at home and come to class with bare wrists, neck and ears.

Although you have to learn how to get dressed for class all by yourself, there's sometimes an assistant in the changing room who can help students to get ready for the lesson. Girls often need a little help putting their hair up.

You have to remember to fold up your normal clothes neatly, so that they won't be creased at the end of the lesson, and then you put on everything that you need for the lesson. The same rule applies at the end of the lesson. When you change back into your normal clothes, you fold up your leotard and tights and pack them away tidily in your bag, with your shoes and the rest of your ballet equipment.

The changing rooms are a place for chatting and joking with your friends, as long as you don't get too excited. So, no shouting or roaring with laughter and certainly no chasing each other or throwing things. A ballerina needs to be composed and focused, right from the moment when she starts preparing for her lesson or rehearsal.

WARMING UP

I'm Zoe's teacher, but please just call me Gimenez. Everyone else does!

In these pages, you'll learn all about the secrets of warming up. A ballerina's muscles are very precious and should not be put under too much stress and strain. This is why the barre is so important for support. But even before that, and before we do any performances on stage too, we always do our stretching exercises.

THE BUTTERFLY: Sitting on the floor, keep your back straight and your knees bent, with the soles of your feet together. Then bounce your knees up and down, up and down, like the wings of a butterfly. If you can get them to touch the floor, that's really good.

THE CAT: Move on to all fours. Arch your back and lower your head. Then bring your head back to look at the ceiling and bend your back downwards. Be as stretchy as a cat.

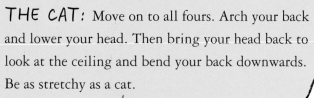

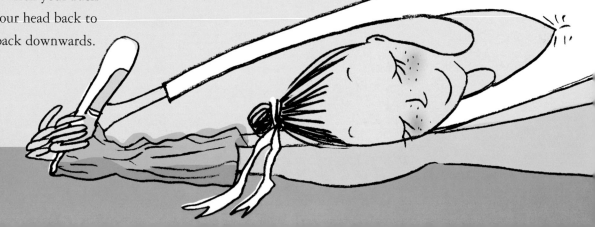

OPEN LEG ROCKER:

This is a rocking exercise that requires both strength and flexibility.

ROLLING LIKE A BALL:

When you roll like a ball, you have to imagine that you're inside a bubble.

TUMMY TRAINER:

You need concentration and control to keep your balance with this exercise!

PILATES

Concentration, body control, fluid movements . . .
Pilates is a special system of exercises that's perfect
for trainee ballerinas. The aim is not to develop the
muscles by doing the same exercise over and over again,
but to link every movement to the one before and to the one
that follows, with complete control of the body and focus on breathing.

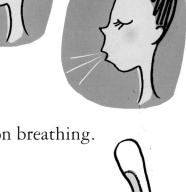

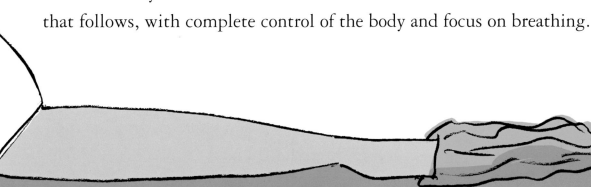

THE BASICS OF BALLET

I'm Laila and I'm half French...

. . . so I'm going to tell you all about the basics of ballet because a lot of the words in dance are French. That's because ballet first became important in France, in the seventeenth century, at the court of Louis XIV, the Sun King. He adored dance and enjoyed dancing himself until he got too old and fat.

THE POSITIONS

Classical ballet is based on the *en dehors* position, the turn-out, with legs and feet pointing outwards. It's quite an awkward position, because it's not natural, but it gives you freedom to move in any direction. Some people are naturally good at this position, even when they're very young, but others find it more difficult. You have to perfect it slowly, a little at a time, by doing exercises that teach the legs to move that way naturally That's why people sometimes say that ballerinas look as though they're double-jointed.

You have to keep your back straight and look right in front of you, with your chin held high and your shoulders low. Try to imagine that you're a puppet with a string in the centre of your head holding you up straight. That's the way a ballerina has to feel.

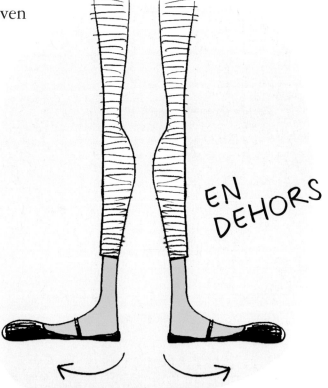

EN DEHORS

There are five basic positions
for the feet and the arms.

SECOND POSITION:
Move your heels apart, but keep your toes turned
out. Hold your arms out to the side, with your
elbows and wrists bent very slightly.

FIRST POSITION:
Keep your heels together,
with your toes turned out.
Your hands should be almost
touching in front of the body.
Hold your arms in an
oval shape.

FOURTH POSITION:
Slide your front foot forward
to create a gap between your
two feet. Raise your front
arm into a rounded position
above your head.

FIFTH POSITION:
Keep your feet close together,
one in front of the other.
Raise both arms into a circle
shape above your head.

THIRD POSITION:
Place your front foot halfway
across your back foot,
with your legs
together. Move one
arm back into first
position.

THE BARRE

The barre is a good friend for anyone studying ballet.

With the support of the barre, you learn your first real exercises, the ones that all ballerinas, even grown-up professional dancers, repeat and repeat every day, for their entire career.

Two barres run parallel along the walls. The rails are at two different heights so that younger dancers and grown-ups have something to support them, no matter how tall or small they are.

PLIÉ:
Bend your knees a little and lower your body, keeping your back straight.

GRAND PLIÉ:
Bend more deeply, with your heels coming off the ground at the end.

GRAND BATTEMENT:
You start with a *battement tendu*, but your toe doesn't stay on the floor – it keeps on going, until it forms a right angle with the body.

BATTEMENT TENDU:
Point your toe and slide your foot out, keeping your toe on the floor.

RELEVÉ:
Go up slowly into *demi-pointe* position, on to the balls of your feet.

ROND-DE-JAMBES:
After a *battement tendu*, move your leg around in a semi-circle, to the front and then back. Then return to the starting position.

RENVERSÉ:
Bend gracefully from the waist, holding one arm in the air. Then return to the starting position.

ARABESQUE:
Lift your leg up behind you as high as you can and lean gently forward.

CENTRE PRACTICE

And finally, after all of that warming up, it's time to step into the centre of the room.

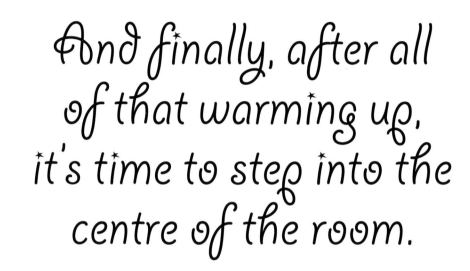

I work with dancers in the studio – my kingdom. It's a big room with the barre running around three sides and a huge mirror covering the fourth wall. The floor is made of wood. There's also a piano, with a pianist who plays to accompany the exercises.

Working in the centre of the room is the most challenging and exciting part of the lesson, the part that's most like real ballet. You practise sequences of steps and short dances. You learn positions and new steps. It is essential to be very strict and precise. I am very serious when it comes to the crucial work of perfecting dance technique.

PAS-DE-CHAT:

This is a jump to the side or the front that imitates the way cats move. The name is actually French for 'cat's step'. The move is very smooth and agile.

GLISSADE:

This is a sliding step that brings both feet together.

WALKING AND RUNNING:

The most simple run is on *demi-pointe*, on the balls of the feet. You move this way when you are making an entrance or taking up position in the centre, or heading back to the barre when it's someone else's turn in the centre of the room. You could also intersperse running steps with jumps and leaps, which looks even more elegant. You can also run *en pointe*, on the very tips of your toes, taking one tiny step after another, but running this way is a skill that only professional dancers should attempt.

GRAND JETÉ:

Throw out the front leg and leap into the air, holding both legs straight as though you are doing the splits. Then land and do the same again.

JUMPS

GRAND JETÉ EN TOURNANT:

This is a jump in which you spin around 180 degrees. You leap up, turn in the air and land on the other foot.

In ballet there are small jumps and big leaps, high jumps and long leaps. Usually you practise at the barre, holding it with both hands, which allows you to lift yourself higher. Then you try it out in the centre of the room, where you have no support at all. You can jump from two legs and land on one leg or both, or start on one and finish on two, start on one leg and finish on the same leg or start on one leg and finish on the other.

ENTRECHAT: Jump into the air and rapidly move one leg in front of the other, once or several times. This has become a typical step for male dancers, although ballerinas were the first to do it.

CHANGEMENT DE PIEDS: Starting from the fifth position, you bend your knees, spring into the air, swap the positions of your feet and then land with knees bent. The foot that was in front to start with is now at the back, and vice versa.

SISSONNE: This is a long leap that is named after the choreographer who invented it. There are different varieties of *sissonne*, which all start on two feet, but end on one or both.

PIROUETTE: To do good pirouettes (spins), you have to learn a technique called 'spotting', which involves focusing on a fixed spot in front you and looking back at that point every time you complete a spin. It's the only way to keep your concentration and your balance.

FOUETTÉ TURN: You start by holding your leg out to one side, then give yourself momentum as you whip the tip of one foot up towards your knee and back again. The impetus spins you around *en pointe* or *demi-pointe*. You carry on like that until you perfect the movement (or collapse in a heap!). Pierina Legnani, a famous Italian ballerina, managed to do thirty-two *fouetté* turns in a row and her feat was included in the choreography for *Swan Lake* in 1895.

CURTSIES AND BOWS: At the end of the lesson in the centre of the room, students thank their teacher with perfect curtsies and bows. This is not just the movement that they will use (one day!) to acknowledge their applauding audience. It's first and foremost a gesture of courtesy, which is, in fact, where the word 'curtsy' comes from.

The mirror is really only there for the best dancers to check how their steps look. Young ballerinas shouldn't spend time looking at themselves in the mirror, but should concentrate on what they're doing!

PAS DE DEUX

This is a dance for experienced ballerinas . . .

. . . who have to perform complex steps with a male partner. The man has to do the lifting (this is one of the reasons why classical ballerinas are almost always so tiny and light – who could lift them otherwise?). He helps the ballerina to balance, jump and pirouette, lifts her up, carries her, accompanies her as she dances across the stage and still has to remember to perform his own movements correctly.

Pas de deux are by far the most wonderful and exciting moments in ballet. The dancers mime first encounters, passion, arguments, reconciliation and moments of complete happiness or despair. When they are on stage, the best ballet dancers move so smoothly as a couple that the audience don't realise how much concentration and effort is required to coordinate all of the movements so beautifully – or even notice the physical exertion of the partner as he lifts the ballerina. Even if she's very light, it's still hard work.

CHARACTER DANCE

I'm Kai Zwerger, one of Zoe's teachers.

I teach character dance, which is all about expression and traditional steps.
It's always been my greatest passion. When I was at school though, I loved mime lessons and pretending to be different animals.

MIME

You usually start to experiment with expressive dance by trying to imitate animals.

Cats and lions move smoothly, slowly,
with that agile feline grace.

You imitate butterflies by running on tiptoe and stopping briefly, as though you're landing on a flower, and fluttering your arms up and down.

Elephants move slowly, with heavy steps.

You can imitate toys as well . . . Here's a line of soldiers. They're marching along, stiff and straight, like proper military men.

This is a mechanical doll. She has a smile painted on her face and she walks with jerking movements. The jack-in-the-box is on a spring, so he pops up out of the box and then bounces from side to side.

EXPRESSIONS

The expressions on your face and the movements of your body are very important when you want to tell a story. You have to communicate emotions with delicacy and clarity. You don't dance just with your legs, but with your eyes, your mouth and the movements of your hands and arms. That may sound a little strange, but it makes sense if you think about it. After all, in everyday life we use the whole of our bodies to express our emotions.

To be a good ballet dancer, it's not enough to have perfect technique and extraordinary athletic ability. You also have to be able to show a wide range of emotions. Otherwise, you run the risk of looking like a skilled puppet with a clever way of working, but no heart.

happiness   sadness   shyness   sorrow   love

FOLK DANCE

Folk dance is very old indeed.
Every culture has its own traditional dances.
Ballet has borrowed a lot of these steps.
The tarantella, the polka, mazurka,
morris dancing – these are just some
examples of folk dances.
Choreographers revisit these steps and
sequences, taking inspiration from
these rich traditions. Dances of this kind are
usually performed in costumes that are inspired by their country of origin:
brightly coloured skirts, velvet bodices, blouses with puff sleeves and special headdresses.

THE TUTU

One day, my little treasures will be allowed to put away their simple outfits and wear proper tutus instead!

We're doing rehearsals for the end-of-year recital at the moment. My little dears are really excited. I can see why, because, even for a grown-up ballerina, trying on a new tutu and finding out how it's going to support and enhance your movements is such an important moment, and it's always very emotional.

I'm Demetra, the costume-maker. I love my job. It feels a bit like giving real substance to dreams. Admittedly, a clumsy ballerina dressed in a beautiful tutu will look like a duckling dressed up in peacock's feathers. It takes more than just a costume to make a star. But the tutu certainly helps!

sequins

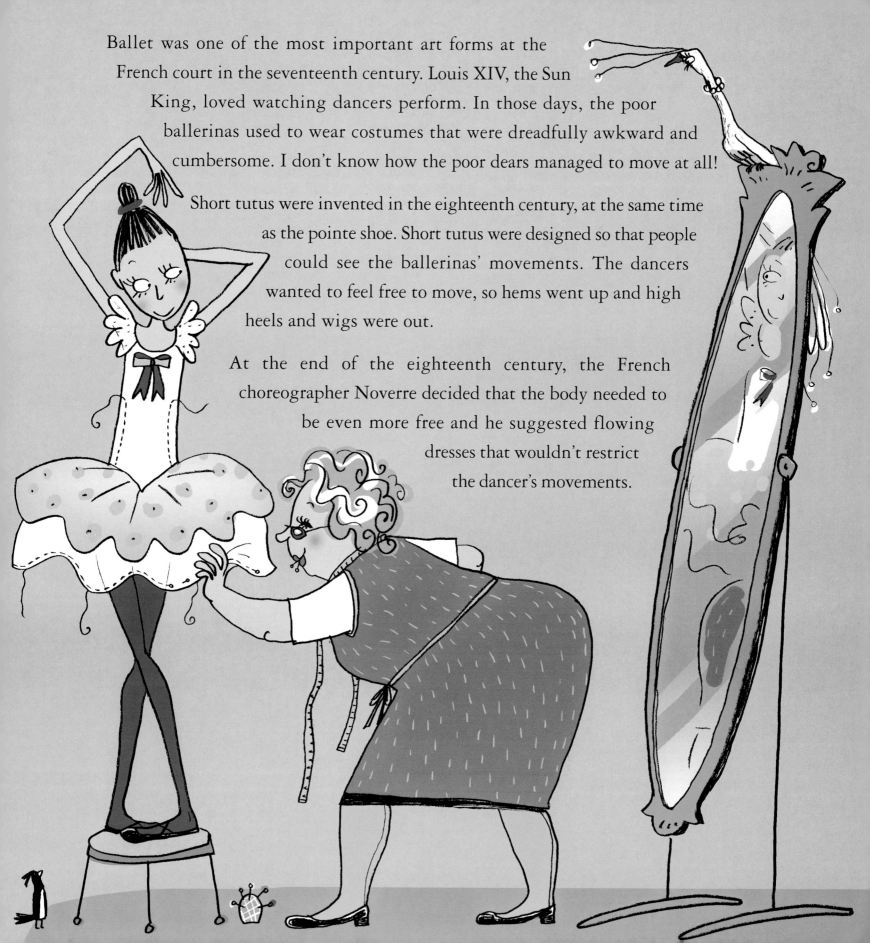

Ballet was one of the most important art forms at the French court in the seventeenth century. Louis XIV, the Sun King, loved watching dancers perform. In those days, the poor ballerinas used to wear costumes that were dreadfully awkward and cumbersome. I don't know how the poor dears managed to move at all!

Short tutus were invented in the eighteenth century, at the same time as the pointe shoe. Short tutus were designed so that people could see the ballerinas' movements. The dancers wanted to feel free to move, so hems went up and high heels and wigs were out.

At the end of the eighteenth century, the French choreographer Noverre decided that the body needed to be even more free and he suggested flowing dresses that wouldn't restrict the dancer's movements.

The first longer tutu was invented in 1832 for a great Italian ballerina, Marie Taglioni, when she danced in the ballet *La Sylphide*. Her tutu was very light and floaty and it went down to her knees. She was dancing the part of a fairy of the forests, a magical and ethereal creature, and her costume had to reflect that. She wore pink pointe shoes and had two little wings sewn on to the back of her bodice.

I would so love to have seen her wear that!

Since then, it's really been a case of 'anything goes': short stiff tutus, long soft ones, costumes inspired by ancient Rome, even spacesuits! The list is endless.

Every theatre has a costume designer, who brings along his or her own ideas for designs. I do what I'm told, like a good costume-maker. Of course, I add my own touches too. Who knows better how a material is going to fall? Or how a particular fabric will look in the harsh lights of the stage?

Of course, some modern materials are so light and shiny that they're perfect for creating miniature works of art to underline the ballerina's graceful movements, even though she is scarcely aware that she's even wearing a costume. And then there are all the headdresses to go with the tutus – tiaras for princesses, bands of feathers for the ballerinas in *Swan Lake*, and so on. I always try to design them so that they're easy for the dancers to wear, and, of course, so that they don't come flying off just at the wrong moment!

Oooh! Now it's time for the performance!
This time we're all on stage!
Come on, everyone! Concentrate!
This has to be perfect!

The end-of-year recital

The end-of-year recital is the time to show everyone what we've learned – not only our technique, but also our ability to express emotions and to perform in public. But anyone who studies dance obviously enjoys performing and can't wait to get on stage!

We rehearse for a few weeks. First, we try out the dance steps piece by piece in the studio. Then we put them all together, linking all of the pieces together. Finally, we move on to the real stage. Ooh, it gives me the shivers just thinking about it! It's like being a real dancer. The theatre has an odd smell – strange, but nice – sort of like dust and wood. And it has so many dark and mysterious corners that it can feel a bit creepy, especially in the wings, with those long red velvet curtains rising up into the darkness way above your head and vanishing in amongst the tangle of cables and scaffolding. There are so many lovely secret places to discover in a theatre.

On the stage there are little circles and crosses made out of fluorescent sticky tape. They mark out the spots so that we can see where to position ourselves, even in the dark, so that the dance looks perfectly arranged to the audience.

We do the rehearsals in our usual dance outfits. When Madame gets annoyed with us and stops the music and makes us start again, it feels just like a normal lesson. But we know that it isn't, and we're even more scared of her temper than we normally are. The dress rehearsal is a different story though. We have to wear our costumes and everything has to go smoothly, with no interruptions, as though it were the actual performance. The idea is to check that there are no problems and to make sure that everyone knows that this is serious. No more joking about – the next time will be for real.

And then, finally, we're ready. It's the big day, the moment everyone's been waiting for. We're in our costumes (and the girls are wearing a touch of make-up) and we've done a few warm-up and barre exercises (on the barre backstage). And we're waiting, huddled together in the wings, in breathless silence. The lights go down in the theatre and the chattering of the audience dies down. Everything falls silent. The music strikes up. And . . . that's it! The first act has begun . . .

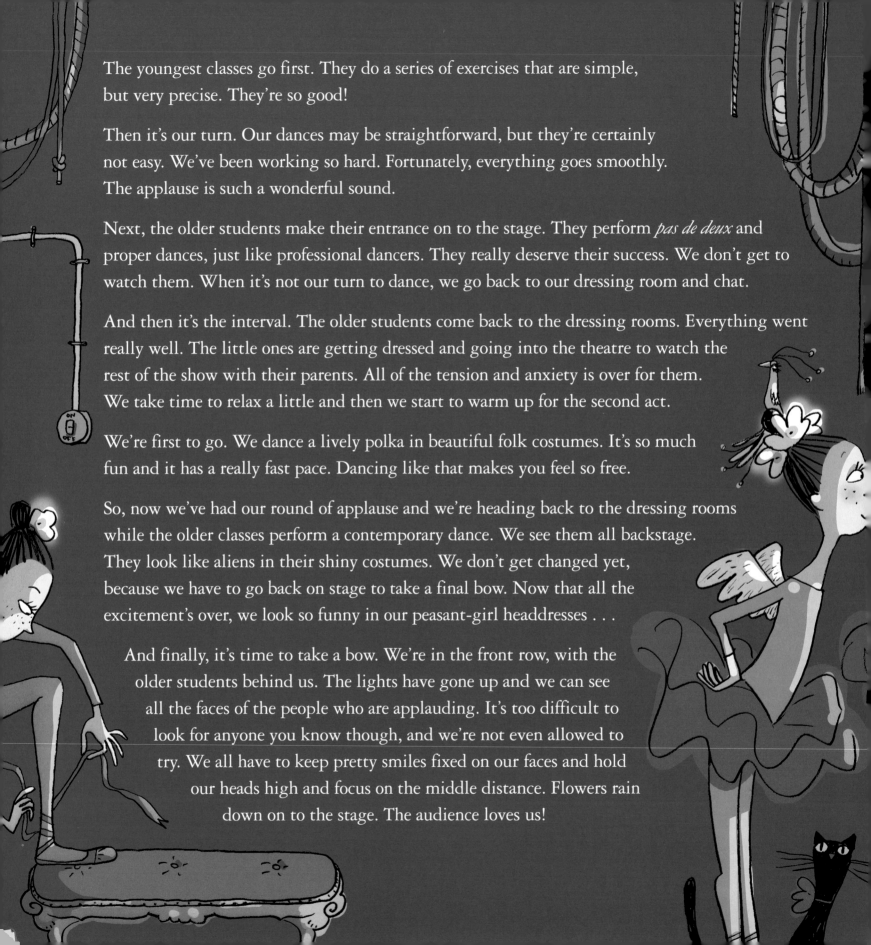

The youngest classes go first. They do a series of exercises that are simple, but very precise. They're so good!

Then it's our turn. Our dances may be straightforward, but they're certainly not easy. We've been working so hard. Fortunately, everything goes smoothly. The applause is such a wonderful sound.

Next, the older students make their entrance on to the stage. They perform *pas de deux* and proper dances, just like professional dancers. They really deserve their success. We don't get to watch them. When it's not our turn to dance, we go back to our dressing room and chat.

And then it's the interval. The older students come back to the dressing rooms. Everything went really well. The little ones are getting dressed and going into the theatre to watch the rest of the show with their parents. All of the tension and anxiety is over for them. We take time to relax a little and then we start to warm up for the second act.

We're first to go. We dance a lively polka in beautiful folk costumes. It's so much fun and it has a really fast pace. Dancing like that makes you feel so free.

So, now we've had our round of applause and we're heading back to the dressing rooms while the older classes perform a contemporary dance. We see them all backstage. They look like aliens in their shiny costumes. We don't get changed yet, because we have to go back on stage to take a final bow. Now that all the excitement's over, we look so funny in our peasant-girl headdresses . . .

And finally, it's time to take a bow. We're in the front row, with the older students behind us. The lights have gone up and we can see all the faces of the people who are applauding. It's too difficult to look for anyone you know though, and we're not even allowed to try. We all have to keep pretty smiles fixed on our faces and hold our heads high and focus on the middle distance. Flowers rain down on to the stage. The audience loves us!

THE GREAT CLASSICAL BALLETS

When music and dance come together ...

. . . they tell the same story in two different languages: the language of music and the language of movements. I'm Maestro Fantin and I'm going to tell you all about the great classic ballets. These are romantic, passionate stories, often amusing, nearly always very emotional, with a large dose of the fantastic. They are the ballets that every classical ballerina dreams of performing one day, when they are a leading dancer.

During the lessons, when the students are practising a section of a classical ballet, I play the simplified version of the full ballet music, just on the piano. It can seem like a completely different piece of music when the orchestra plays it! But the charm of the great ballets is irresistible, even when the music is played by a single piano.

CINDERELLA

Music by Sergei Prokofiev

This is a faithful retelling of the traditional fairytale.
A good daughter, two stepsisters and a stepmother, a fairy godmother gifted with extraordinary powers, a ball, the clock striking twelve, a glass shoe being lost . . . and a happy ending.

The composer said about his opera, 'What I wished to express above all in the music of *Cinderella* was the poetic love of Cinderella and the Prince, the birth and flowering of that love, the obstacles in its path and finally the dream fulfilled.'

An interesting fact is that the parts of the stepmother and the stepsisters in this ballet are traditionally set aside for male dancers dressed as women. They look really silly, of course, but the idea is to make fun of the nastiest people in this story.

SWAN LAKE

Music by Pyotr Ilyich Tchaikovsky

Prince Siegfried falls in love with the beautiful Odette, who has been cursed by the sorcerer Rothbart to turn into a swan during the daytime. The spell will be broken only if Odette is truly loved. The prince decides to present Odette to his mother as his future wife, but the sorcerer finds out. He imprisons Odette and visits the court himself, together with Odile, his daughter, who appears identical to Odette, except she is dressed in black, while Odette is in white. Rothbart's spell makes the prince believe that Odile is Odette and he promises to marry her.

Odette flees in despair. When Siegfried discovers that he has been deceived, he follows her. Rothbart conjures up a storm to destroy the lovers, but their love triumphs and defeats the evil spell. It must have taken a powerful enchantment for Siegfried to confuse sweet Odette with the dark and sinister Odile . . . but in fairytales, of course, anything is possible.

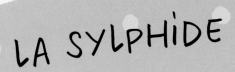

LA SYLPHIDE

Music by Jean-Madeleine Schneitzhoeffer

This ballet was created for a ballerina, Marie Taglioni, daughter of the choreographer Filippo Taglioni, who invented a dance technique specially for her: dancing *en pointe*, on the very tips of the toes. Marie Taglioni danced the ballet for the first time in 1832 in Paris, wearing a white knee-length tutu. The story is set in Scotland and it includes fairies and witches in its cast of characters.

La Sylphide is a sylph, a forest fairy, and she enchants James, who is engaged to marry Effie, and steals his engagement ring, forcing him to run after her. The witch Madge creates a magic scarf and tells James to throw it around the sylph's neck to bind her to him and stop her flying away. He does as he is told, but the magical creature dies. In the meantime, Effie is consoled by James's friend Gurn, who has always loved her. Effie and Gurn marry, and poor James remains alone and unhappy.

THE NUTCRACKER

Music by Pyotr Ilyich Tchaikovsky

Based on the story by E.T.A. Hoffmann, this is the tale of Clara,

who receives a gift from her godfather Herr Drosselmeyer on Christmas Eve.

It's a wooden nutcracker in the shape of a soldier...

GISELLE

Music by Adolphe Adam

Count Albrecht, disguised as a peasant, flirts with the beautiful

peasant girl Giselle, and makes her fall in love with him.

But he is already engaged to be married to a noblewoman, and the gamekeeper

Hilarion, who is in love with Giselle, tries in vain to warn her.

When Giselle discovers the truth, she loses her mind and kills herself.

ROMEO AND JULIET

Music by Sergei Prokofiev

This is Shakespeare's drama transformed into a ballet,

telling the story of the two star-crossed young lovers from Verona,

whose love is thwarted by a family feud.

They story ends with both of them dying tragically.

STARS OF YESTERDAY AND TODAY

I have a secret passion for the history of ballet and the great people who have played a part in it.

I love cutting out pictures of famous figures from ballet history and sticking them into my diary. Not just photos, but pictures of paintings too, of all the great ballerinas – the ones who lived in the days before everyone had a camera.

They're old-style pictures and they show the ballerinas as delicate, magical creatures, who scarcely seem real. In comparison, the pictures of the great dancers of today look so aggressive. But then a lot has changed in the world of dance. It's nice to compare the past with the present and to see just how many different aspects there are to ballet and its history.

WEDS 2

Today:
Cost
Fit

10:00

LEDAV

Rain Today

music
geography
ssons

MARIE TAGLIONI

A great romantic ballerina, born in Stockholm, Taglioni was taught to dance by her father, who was a choreographer. She was the star of the ballet *La Sylphide*, which was written especially for her, and she first danced it in 1832. She had every capital city in Europe at her feet.

Today I'm 1.73m tall!

LOVE

Lesson

It's Sunny

FANNY ELSSLER

Fanny Elssler was Marie Taglioni's great rival. She studied dance in Naples in the nineteenth century and enjoyed huge success in major cities such as Berlin and Vienna. She danced in Russia and went on tour to the United States and Cuba (and don't forget that it wasn't as easy to travel in those days). Compared with Taglioni, who was as light and delicate as a forest fairy, she danced in a more sensual and passionate way. Nearly all of the portraits of Elssler show her dressed in a Spanish style. I think she was probably a bit like Gimenez.

FRI 27

Full moon

ANNA PAVLOVA

Anna Pavlova started studying dance in Saint Petersburg when she was ten years old and joined the Imperial Ballet at the Mariinsky Theatre at the age of eighteen. A wonderful dancer, she toured the world, performing in all of the major theatres.
In 1905, she became the first ballerina to perform *The Dying Swan*, a solo dance created for her by the choreographer Fokine, which was based on her ability to express the fluttering wings of a dying swan with her arms. In 1914, she decided not to return to her homeland and settled in Europe.

12.30 – Lunch with friends

VASLAV NIJINSKIJ

The son of two Polish dancers, Nijinsky became famous in Paris, where he danced with Diaghilev's Ballets Russes, and went on to create his own choreography. In 1912, he choreographed and danced an extraordinary, original performance based on Debussy's *Prélude à l'après-midi d'un faune.* Absolutely magnificent!

She danced in bare feet

ISADORA DUNCAN

Born in San Francisco, Isadora Duncan abandoned the tutu and pointe shoes and invented a style of dance that was inspired by Ancient Greece. Her style was more natural and instinctive and she danced in bare feet. She died in 1927 in Nice, strangled by her long white scarf, when it became entangled in the wheels of the car she was in.

→ revise history

me →

10am-Pilates

RUDOLF NUREYEV

Rudolf Nureyev was a brilliant dancer from the Kirov Ballet in Leningrad. In 1961, when he was on a tour of Europe, he asked France for political asylum, so that he did not have to return to the Soviet Union, where dancers had little opportunity for experimentation and invention. Several of his fellow dancers did the same. Nureyev died in 1993. As a dancer and a choreographer, he is unforgettable.

MARGOT FONTEYN

The star of British dance, Fonteyn often danced with Nureyev as her partner. They made an extraordinary couple.

MIKHAIL BARYSHNIKOV

Like Nureyev, he left the Kirov while he was on tour in Canada, and then settled in the United States. The star and artistic director of the American Ballet Theatre, he has also appeared in a number of successful films and television shows, most of which are about the world of dance. I absolutely love them!

my hero

Today I saw a rainbow WOW!

Party today

CARLA FRACCI

The diva of Italian dance. She studied ballet as a little girl at the ballet school of La Scala in Milan and became prima ballerina there in 1958. She has danced in all of the world's most important theatres.

DARCEY BUSSELL

One of the greatest English dancers of all time. She did not start studying ballet seriously until she was thirteen, but went on to become the youngest dancer to be awarded the role of prima ballerina at the The Royal Ballet in London, where she studied.

MAXIMILIANO GUERRA & JULIO BOCCA

These two dancers both come from Argentina. They share the same strength and skill too. What's more, they're very handsome and they're popular with audiences all over the world, particularly the women!

ADAM COOPER

Adam Cooper is a young, talented English dancer who became really popular (but he was already very famous before then) when he appeared in the final scenes of the film *Billy Elliot*. He plays Billy as an adult when he performs on stage in a contemporary performance of *Swan Lake*, which features only male dancers.

9am - Gimenez

Wonderful dream last night - I was dancing with Adam Cooper!

Leda loves

Gorgeous

ROBERTO BOLLE

Roberto Bolle joined the La Scala dance school at a very young age and was fifteen when Nureyev saw him performing a barre exercise and chose him to perform the role of Tadzio, the beautiful adolescent, in the ballet *Death in Venice*. He became lead male dancer at La Scala at a young age and this was the start of an international career that took him to theatres all over the world. In January 2006, he performed a dance that was choreographed just for him at the opening ceremony of the Winter Olympics in Turin.

Only 20 days until the final performance - gulp!

LOVE

CONTEMPORARY DANCE

You still have to train in classical ballet . . .

. . . if you want to explore contemporary dance when you grow up and perhaps even invent your own way of expressing yourself through dance.

In contemporary dance, the body is free to experiment with every possible type of movement, and be fearless and daring, and always expressive. Contemporary dance is all about people today, their stories, their fears and their passions.

Many different dancers and companies have contributed to the development of contemporary dance. I'm going to tell you about just a few of my favourites.

JOSÉ LIMÓN

'I believe that we are never more truly and profoundly human than when we dance.' That's a nice quote, isn't it? It's something that José Limón said. He was born in Mexico, but moved to America as an adult, where he founded his own dance company in 1946 with his teacher Doris Humphrey. Concentration, clean and pure gestures and movements, great expression: these are the key features of the Limón method.

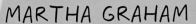

MARTHA GRAHAM

Martha Graham, an American dancer and choreographer, founded her own company in 1929. Her mission was to draw a 'graph of the heart' through movement. For a long time, she was the principal performer in the dances that she choreographed, which are violent, disturbing and dramatic. She said of her style, 'I did not want it to be beautiful or fluid. I wanted it to be fraught with inner meaning, with excitement and surge.'

ROLAND PETIT

Petit started as a dancer, then founded his own company, the Ballets de Marseille, in 1972. He is French and has never forgotten the importance of academic dance in his work, happily mixing it with the style of the music hall.

MAURICE BÉJART

Béjart founded the Ballet du XXe siècle in Brussels and then moved his dance company to Switzerland (the Béjart Ballet Lausanne). He also founded the Mudra dance school, which started in Belgium, but also has a base in Africa, and then he changed the name to Rudra. He was a man full of energy and imagination. His dance was also about theatre, song and drama. Everything comes together to tell a story for — and about — human beings.

PINA BAUSCH

Pina Bausch invented Tanztheater, which means 'dance theatre' in German, the language she speaks. The dancers improvise with her and then join their pieces together, with the aim of telling the stories, the passions and the pain, of people today.

MOMIX

And then there's Momix . . . They're dancers, but they're also a bit like mime artists and a bit like magicians. They play with their bodies, transforming them into amazing objects. Your jaw drops in amazement as they turn into flowers, plants and strange shapes, shifting and changing before your very eyes. The man who started Momix is called Moses Pendleton and he was a skier before founding the Pilobolus Dance Theatre, his first dance company, with a friend, and then going on to found Momix in 1988. I think they're absolutely fantastic!

DANCE IN ART

Over the past two hundred years, many painters and sculptors have captured the spirit of dance in their art . . .

Edgar Degas believed that art had to represent reality, so he visited a lot of dance lessons in order to learn how to depict the ballerinas and their world as accurately as possible, both in his paintings and in his sculptures. He worked in France in the second half of the nineteenth century.

In the early twentieth century, Henri Matisse worked for the Ballets Russes in Paris, where he designed sets. And so dance entered into his paintings, which depict the fluidity of movement.

Realist
ballerina

Futurist
ballerina

Fortunato Depero, an Italian Futurist artist, also worked for the Ballets Russes. He liked puppets and geometric designs.

Pablo Picasso, a Cubist painter, had his own way of seeing reality and used his art to dismantle what he saw. And, of course, he treated dancers in the same way.

Keith Haring, a young American artist, worked in New York in the 1970s and 80s. He often depicted figures performing street dance, the kind of dancing that people do on street corners with the volume on their ghetto-blaster turned way up high.

Cubist
ballerina

WORKING IN THE WORLD OF DANCE

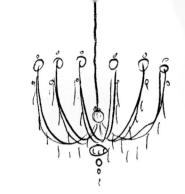

The world of dance has lots of interesting job opportunities to offer.

Anyone who is interested in the world of dance and theatre will find that there are lots of ways to become part of it by using your technical and artistic skills on the stage – and elsewhere in the theatre.

THE TEACHER

First you have to graduate from a major dance school, then you take courses in how to teach and finally you can start work as a dance teacher. There are lots of different options – there's not only classical ballet, but also character dance, contemporary dance, and many other forms that you can specialise in.

THE COSTUME-MAKER

A theatrical costume-maker sews costumes, of course, and works in close collaboration with the costume designer, but also has to understand the materials and the history of the many different styles that have been used in the past, in order to find sources of inspiration and devise new and original creations.

THE ACCOMPANIST

The accompanist plays the piano for ballerinas to dance to when they're studying or rehearsing.

THE HAIRDRESSER AND MAKE-UP ARTIST

The theatrical hairdresser learns how to do not only hairstyles, but also wigs and hairpieces, moustaches and beards, for all of the different characters in the show. The make-up artist (who is sometimes the same person as the hairdresser) creates a look to emphasise the character that the performer is playing. To do this job, you also need to study the history of theatre and costumes.

THE CHOREOGRAPHER

The choreographer is the person who 'designs' the ballet by deciding on the sequence of steps that should go with the music so that the story is expressive and meaningful. The same piece of music can be designed in very different ways. A dancer like Nureyev, for example, created lots of new choreography for musical works that had already become ballets in the past. The choreographer has often had a career as a dancer or works as both a dancer and a choreographer. After all, who knows better than a dancer how to express ideas and emotions through gestures and movements?

THE THEATRE PHOTOGRAPHER

Photographing a ballet and its performers is not an easy task. You're working indoors, with people who are constantly moving and standing in unnatural lighting. You have to be able to capture individual moments and expressions, specific movements and group scenes.

THE STAGEHAND

The stagehand is a technician who works on stage and knows how to assemble, dismantle and move the various sets for a show. The stagehand has to be completely familiar with the stage and understand how sets are constructed and how to use the secret mechanisms that make the scenery change as if by magic.

THE LIGHTING TECHNICIAN

The lighting technician combines artistic skills and technical knowledge to illuminate the show, and works at the lighting desk, the control centre for all of the lights in the theatre.

THE SET AND COSTUME DESIGNER

Creating the sets and costumes for a theatrical show, an opera or a ballet is a fascinating job. To learn how to do it, you have to study history, analyse the great shows of the past and the present, and then gain practical experience by watching and helping to design sets and costumes. Much of the set designer's work is done on computers nowadays.

HOPES AND DREAMS

Hmm, I've already told you all there is to know about me. So, my friends are going to talk to you and tell you all about what they want to do – and don't want to do – when they're older. And my grown-up friends can tell you a few of their secrets too . . .

Right now, all I want to do is stop growing. I'm worried I will be too tall for classical dancing. I can't make myself any shorter, but it would be good if I could stop growing at least!

My biggest wish – everyone's biggest wish – is to become a leading dancer. I know that I have a lot of work to do, for years and years. But I'm ready to do it.

I want to be a choreographer. That's what interests me most. So I'll complete my dance course and get my qualifications, then I'll specialise and go and study abroad, and then work with a major company of brilliant dancers.

Well, after all that I told you about the stars of contemporary dance, it's clear what I want to do when I'm older! I want to work for a big contemporary dance company for a while. And then I'll go on to do my own thing.

Do you think a little old man like me doesn't have any dreams? Well, you're wrong. I want a talented young person to inherit my position, someone who really enjoys playing for the youngest ballet dancers. You learn so much from them, and they're such fun to work with. As for me, I dream of taking a bouquet to one of my little friends in their dressing room after their magnificent debut.

I had some problems a while back – I thought I wasn't thin enough, and I wanted to get even thinner. Now I know that I was just being silly, and I've realised something very important: I can only dance if I'm feeling well, if I'm full of energy. Otherwise, I can't dance. And I mustn't forget that.

The Academy is my baby, as it has been for all of the other heads of the school before me. Each of us has added something of our own to it and created a piece of this wonderful history – the history of a great theatre and a great dance academy famous throughout the world. I hope to continue to train dancers who will make the whole world go wild with applause.

THE WORLD'S GREAT DANCE SCHOOLS

All the schools work in more or less the same way.

Some of them have introductory courses for children from the age of six to ten to prepare them to study dance. The children learn how to follow a rhythm, how to listen to music, how to understand their own bodies and use them with confidence. The lessons are very strict and demanding, but the teachers never forget the importance of play.

THE ENTRANCE EXAM

Proper dance courses begin at around the age of ten or eleven, following an entrance exam, which is partly medical and partly to do with aptitude. The medical exam is an orthopaedic check to make sure that the aspiring ballet dancer's body is suitable for dance. There are physical requirements that are necessary for anyone who wants to take up dance seriously, such as elasticity, the body's natural ability to perform certain movements that we don't do in everyday life. The aptitude test is to see whether the prospective student has a talent for music and a good sense of rhythm, which you need if you want to move in time with the music. Usually, around fifteen to twenty candidates are accepted at a dance academy each year from hundreds of applicants.

Right from day one, the courses are very serious and demanding. The morning is usually set aside for dance exercises in the studio. Then, in the early afternoon, the young dancers move to a proper classroom. Their education is never neglected, even though the focus in dance schools is obviously on dance and everything that's related to dancing.

While the ordinary school subjects are more or less the same as in every other school, students at dance schools also have lessons about basic dance techniques. They have lessons in dance theory and history too, because you have to know about what happened in the past in order to be a good dancer in the present. And it's important to know more about music than the casual listener. You really have to study music and understand it on a deeper level.

A lot of time is also devoted to physical education, which is of course designed to strengthen the body in ways that are most helpful for dancers, so there's a lot of stretching and you learn Pilates too.

A week containing all of these different subjects is obviously a very busy week indeed! This means that young ballerinas have to be very dedicated and have strong willpower. Some people find out very quickly that they're not suited to this routine. But there are also lots of students who grit their teeth and carry on.

Subjects

Classical ballet
Character dance
Contemporary dance
Repertoire
Pas de deux
Gymnastics
Irish and Scottish dancing
History of ballet
History of music
Theory and musical analysis

SELECTION

At the end of every year, or after a set number of years (it depends on the school), the students have to pass an exam before they can move into the next year, to show that they have learned everything that was expected of them.

The selection procedure also opens at the end of every year for students who have come from other dance academies and want to join the school.

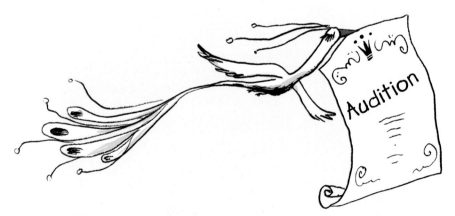

AND THEN . . .

After many years of study (it's eight years at the Academy, plus five years in the junior section), you have to take your final exam.

Qualified dancers can take part in the auditions that the world's biggest ballet companies regularly hold to select new dancers.
These are some of the greatest ballet companies in the world.

TEATRO ALLA SCALA

In 1776, a fire destroyed the Teatro Regio Ducale di Milano in Italy. So Empress Maria Theresa of Austria decided to have a new theatre for opera and ballet built on the site where the church of Santa Maria alla Scala had previously stood. The theatre was designed by the architect Piermarini and inaugurated in 1778. The dance school opened in the early nineteenth century. Now it is called the Accademia d'Arti e Mestieri dello Spettacolo and every year it produces many graduates in different theatrical disciplines.

ROYAL BALLET SCHOOL

This school is in London and it was founded in 1926. It has two different sections: a lower school for students from 11 to 16, and an upper school for students from 16 to 18.

SCHOOL OF AMERICAN BALLET

This is the school connected to the New York City Ballet. It's based at the Lincoln Center, in the heart of New York. It was founded in 1934 by the choreographer George Balanchine and it accepts students from the age of 8 to 18.

THE BOLSHOI

This is Moscow's great historic theatre, and the school connected to it has produced extraordinarily talented artists.

THE KIROV

This is the theatre of Saint Petersburg and it has a history of over two hundred years in the tradition of ballet.

OPÉRA DE PARIS

The dance school of the most famous theatre in Paris will be three hundred years old in 2013. It was established by King Louis XIV. The school now takes boys and girls from the age of 8, who have to follow a six-month introductory course before being officially admitted (or a year-long course for children of 10 and over) to make sure that they're suited to the discipline of dance.

Here we are, all together again!

So, we've told you all about ballet from lots of different points of view and now we'd like to say farewell with elegant bows and curtsies, as we do at the end of a performance. But our individual stories will continue, and so will our hard work, our patience and our passion for a beautiful art: dance.

Share the life and dreams of Zoe and her dancer friends at Ballet Academy!

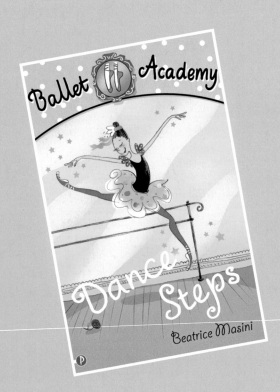

Dance Steps
Beatrice Masini

A Question of Character
Beatrice Masini

Friends Old and New
Beatrice Masini

More books to come!